WORKING OUT THE COVENANT

A Shared Spiritual Heritage

Gillian Kingston

Published by
Church of Ireland Publishing
Church of Ireland House
Church Avenue
Rathmines, Dublin 6

www.cip.ireland.anglican.org

Designed by Susan Hood

ISBN 978-1-904884-25-5

Printed by Paceprint Trading Ltd,
Dublin, Ireland

Table of Contents

Foreword

AS CO-CHAIRS OF THE COVENANT COUNCIL OF the Church of Ireland and the Methodist Church in Ireland, it gives us great pleasure to commend this compilation of some of the spiritual treasures we share. Here you will find reference to hymns which can be found in each of our hymnals, along with prayers hallowed by tradition, but ever fresh in their comfort and application to the Christian pilgrimage. And there are resources for exploring together the concept of Covenant relationship, both with God and with each other.

As we journey forward in the spirit of the Covenant, it is our hope that this booklet will contribute to our understanding of the closeness of our historic links as traditions within the One Church, and of the richness of our shared heritage in history, spirituality and liturgy.

This is the third in a series of publications by the Covenant Council which seeks to enlarge our understanding of each other. Our divided family is being drawn toward fuller communion by our common heritage and our desire to be one in worship, mission and witness.

Most Revd Richard Clarke, Church of Ireland Bishop of Meath and Kildare

Revd David Kerr, former President, Methodist Church in Ireland

1
Introduction

ON A WET THURSDAY AFTERNOON in September 2002, a group of some 25 people met at Chrome Hill House, outside Lisburn, County Antrim. They stood together at the foot of two trees joined half way up the trunk and growing together as one – a strange, but natural, phenomenon symbolising the significance of the meeting. They sang a hymn, listened to the word of God and prayed, then proceeded indoors to sign a covenant pledging themselves to work more closely together as people of God in this land.

The working out of the Covenant between the Church of Ireland and the Methodist Church in Ireland began with a shared act of worship – praising God, acknowledging past failings and looking to the future with hope and joy. As a tribute to the sentiment of that important occasion when the Covenant was signed, we have reproduced the text of the service in the Appendix to this booklet.

It had seemed natural to those planning the event that this should be the case – Methodist and Church of Ireland people, as with Methodist and Anglican people around the world, have a shared spiritual heritage; they each have further riches they can share with each other in a new covenant relationship.

This third booklet in the series *Working out the Covenant*, invites the Churches to explore something of that heritage, shared and individual, and offers ways of continuing the journey in a spirit of worship and praise.

Included are prayers for unity from the prayer books of both Churches and which are in current use in those Churches; Wesley Day (24 May) collects from each Church; treasures in prayer for Christian unity from other sources; and prayers from the Wesleyan tradition, entitled 'Praying with the Wesleys' (contributed by the Revd Dudley Levistone Cooney, formerly co-Chair of the Joint Theological Working Party, to whom the Covenant Council is deeply indebted). The hymns of Charles and John Wesley common to the hymnals of both Churches are discussed in detail in the chapter devoted to Wesley hymns, again contributed by Mr Levistone Cooney, who explores the context and content of each of these. The text of the Methodist Covenant Service and the Covenant between the two Churches are further provided for reference and complete the volume.

In 2006, the General Synod of the Church of Ireland and the Methodist Conference received the following recommendation from the Covenant Council:

> The Council wants to encourage a time of celebration both of the Covenant and of our common heritage around September 26th each year the anniversary of the signing of the Covenant. Material which might be used for such an event will be collated and made available both on the proposed website and in hard copy. A set order of service is not envisaged, but rather the provision of a theme and related resources. The Council urges that local congregations take this opportunity to worship and celebrate together.

The Council continues to urge Churches to take every opportunity to worship together. In this way, we get to know each other, and are thus better enabled to share each other's riches, to broaden our experience of how God works among his people and to proclaim the Gospel as partners together in God's mission in this land.

The Council is aware that, in many places, Methodist and Church of Ireland people do meet to worship together on a regular basis, whether on special occasions like Harvest festivals or Carol services, and for annual events such as Week of Prayer for Christian Unity or World Day of Prayer services. In many places, Methodist and Church of Ireland people also come together for services during Holy Week. There are services of prayer for healing where liturgies have been developed appropriate to the place and need.

In a number of places, congregations gather simply *in the spirit of the Covenant* to worship in each other's churches and to share each other's liturgies. They worship together because they want to worship together – and do not necessarily need a 'special occasion'. Many more would like to do so, but may not be quite sure how to go about setting this up. The Council would find it helpful to receive any available orders of service to pass on as examples of what may be done in this respect. Please send these to the Honorary Secretary whose contact details will be in the Church of Ireland Directory and the Minutes of Conference of the Methodist Church in Ireland.

In his *Reading in St John's Gospel (first and second series)*, the renowned teacher and preacher the Most Revd William Temple (Archbishop of Canterbury 1942-44) declared that:

Worship is the submission of all our nature to God. It is the quickening of conscience by his holiness; the nourishment of mind with his truth; the purifying of imagination by his beauty; the opening of the heart to his love; the surrender of will to his purpose—and all of this gathered up in adoration, the most selfless emotion of which our nature is capable and therefore the chief remedy for that self-centeredness which is our original sin and the source of all actual sin.

This seems an appropriate perspective from which to view the spiritual heritage shared by the Methodist Church in Ireland and the Church of Ireland and from which to join in worship together as the people of God.

Some thoughts

Arranging a joint service requires both sensitivity and careful planning. A number of issues should be considered, some of which are obvious, while others are not so obvious:

- date and time
- location
- presiding priest/minister at worship
- preacher/speaker
- music, especially hymns and tunes familiar to both congregations
- dress
- follow-up

The Council would want to refer those planning a joint act of worship to the second booklet in this series: *Guidelines for the Journey* (2008), where various areas needing special attention are outlined.

Sharing our spiritual heritage is not just about celebrating what we have in common, such as for example, the hymns of Charles Wesley. It is also about what we may have to offer each other from our different traditions from the time when we have been separate from each other. At the signing of the Covenant between the Methodist Church in Great Britain and the Church of England in November 2006, the Archbishop of Canterbury, the Most Revd Rowan Williams, commented that:

> Just over two centuries ago, the insensitivity and missionary sluggishness of the Church of England provoked a dramatic act of protest from John Wesley; and our two families began to grow apart. Yet in those centuries of separation, don't we have to say that both of our Church communities have been given gifts and have learned lessons that we might not have learned or received had this never happened? As we now take this significant step in our growing together again, we do so not in the pretence that two hundred years have been wasted, or that we can go back to where we were. We have all, in the intervening years, discovered things about Christ and his Kingdom that we are now eager to share with each other, as brothers and sisters working to overcome the distant legacy of arrogance and resentment.

Church of Ireland people might want to share the riches of some of the following:

- the 2004 Book of Common Prayer
- the hymns of great Anglican hymn writers such as George Herbert, John M. Neale or Bishop Timothy Dudley Smith

Methodist people might want to offer some of the following:

- the Covenant Service
- the Methodist tradition of spontaneous prayer (demanding, at its best, careful preparation!)
- the hymns of more recent Methodists like Fred Pratt Green

There are still those who sit in the pews of our respective Churches who have rarely – perhaps never – experienced the <u>regular</u> Sunday worship of the sister Church. The Council encourages an active 'getting to know each other' process. This process should include experiencing the regular worshipping style and liturgy of both Churches, as well as the specially prepared 'joint' services.

Preconceived ideas may need to be dispelled *and* careless worship practice tidied up on occasions when we meet each other at worship. As we receive the honoured guest, we inevitably look at ourselves with fresh eyes to reflect on how we have done things and whether or not we have been true to ourselves at our best.

One way in which congregations might familiarize themselves with each other's worship is to engage in a regular exchange of people reading the Scripture lessons.

Each of our Churches has experience of movements within itself of 'fresh expression,' 'new ways of doing Church', or whatever. We thus face similar challenges and issues as we try to be faithful both to Gospel and to church tradition (in the positive and proper sense of that term) in the twenty-first century.

In all this, the Covenant Council recognises that the two Churches are unevenly spread throughout the island. There are places where Church of Ireland people do not have Methodist neighbours in church terms – and there are places where one Methodist congregation may have a number of Church of Ireland congregations within its 'catchment area.' But where there is a will, there is a way, and this booklet aims to provide a source of reference for worship and praise together, for those willing to try to find that way.

I am most grateful to the Revd Dudley Levistone Cooney for his contributions to the text in this booklet; to the Venerable Ricky Rountree of the Church of Ireland Liturgical Advisory Committee for his advice; and to Susan Hood, Church of Ireland Publications Officer, for editorial guidance and overseeing the publishing project.

Gillian Kingston,
Roscrea, April 2009

2
Prayers for Unity

IN THE PRAYER BOOKS of each of our Churches,
there are both prayers for the unity of God's people, and in celebration and thanks for the ministries of John and Charles Wesley:

Lord Jesus Christ,
who said to your apostles
Peace I leave with you, my peace I give to you:
look not on our sins, but on the faith of your Church,
and grant it the peace and unity of your kingdom;
where you are alive and reign with the Father
and the Holy Spirit, one God, now and for ever. **Amen**

Eternal God and Father,
whose Son at supper prayed that his disciples might be one,
as he is one with you:
Draw us closer to him,
that in common love and obedience to you we may be united to
one another
in the fellowship of the one Spirit,
that the world may believe that he is Lord,
to your eternal glory
through Jesus Christ our Lord. **Amen**

*(The Calendar and Collects according to the use of the
Church of Ireland, 2001)*

Lord God, we thank you for calling us
into the company of those who trust in Christ
and seek to obey his will.
May your Spirit guide and strengthen us
in mission and service to your world;
for we are strangers no longer
but pilgrims together on the way to your kingdom;
through Jesus Christ our Lord. **Amen.**

God of all,
through the gift of your Spirit
you have united your people
in the confession of your name.
Lead us by the same Spirit,
to show to the whole earth
one mind in faith
and one faith for justice;
through Jesus Christ our Lord. **Amen**

(Methodist Worship Book, 1999)

Collects for Wesley Day (24 May annually)

Almighty God,
you raised up your servants, John and Charles Wesley,
to proclaim anew the gift of redemption
and the life of holiness.
Pour out your Holy Spirit,
and revive your work among us;
that inspired by the same faith,
and upheld by the same grace in word and sacrament,
we and all your children may be made one
in the unity of your Church on earth,
even as in heaven we are made one in you;
through Jesus Christ our Lord. **Amen**

(Methodist Worship Book, 1999)

John and Charles Wesley
Evangelists, Hymn Writers, 1791 and 1788

God of mercy,
who inspired John and Charles Wesley
with zeal for your gospel:
grant to all people boldness to proclaim your word
and a heart ever to rejoice in singing your praises;
through Jesus Christ your Son our Lord,
who is alive and reigns with you,
in the unity of the Holy Spirit,
one God, now and for ever.

(*Common Worship*, 2000)

3

Treasures in Prayer

Jesus, where'er thy people meet,
There they behold thy mercy seat;
Where'er they seek thee, thou art found,
And every place is hallowed ground.

William Cowper (1731-1800)
from *Hymns and Psalms* 549; *Church Hymnal* 336

WHENEVER PEOPLE HAVE MET TO WORSHIP and pray, there have been words, phrases, and whole prayers, which have imprinted themselves on their minds and which come back in at times of joy or hardship, pain or trial, to bring comfort and peace. Many are likely to be Collects –prayers of the gathered people of God, 'collected' into short and memorable phrases.

Some are included here, others will arise from the experience of the praying community. And it may be that the traditional and time-honoured language of the Church provides a particular comfort not always afforded by more modern paraphrasing. Methodist people will know that John Wesley knew, used and loved many of these words.

Collect for Purity

Almighty God,
 unto whom all hearts are open,
 all desires known,
and from whom no secrets are hidden,
cleanse the thoughts of our hearts
by the inspiration of your Holy Spirit,
 that we may perfectly love you,
and worthily magnify your holy Name;
through Christ our Lord. Amen.
(*Book of Common Prayer*, 2004)

A General Thanksgiving

Almighty God, Father of all mercies,
we thine unworthy servants
do give thee most humble and hearty thanks
for all thy goodness and loving-kindness
to us and to all men.
We bless thee for our creation, preservation,
and all the blessings of this life;
but above all for thine inestimable love
in the redemption of the world by our Lord Jesus Christ;
for the means of grace, and for the hope of glory.
And, we beseech thee,
give us that due sense of all thy mercies,
that our hearts may be unfeignedly thankful;
and that we show forth thy praise,
not only with our lips, but in our lives,
by giving up our selves to thy service,
and by walking before thee
in holiness and righteousness all our days;
through Jesus Christ our Lord,
to whom, with thee and the Holy Spirit,
be all honor and glory, world without end. Amen.
(*Book of Common Prayer,* 2004)

A Prayer of Confession
Let us confess our sins to God.

Most merciful God,
we confess that we have sinned against you
in thought and word and deed.
We have not loved you with our whole heart.
We have not loved our neighbours as ourselves.

[Silence]

In your mercy,
forgive what we have been,
help us to amend what we are,
and direct what we shall be;
that we may delight in your will

20

and walk in your ways;
through Jesus Christ our Lord. Amen.
from Holy Communion during Ordinary Seasons -First Service,
in the *Methodist Worship Book 1999*)

Collect on the Scriptures

Blessed Lord,
who caused all holy Scriptures to be written for our learning:
help us to hear them,
to read, mark, learn and inwardly digest them
that, through patience, and the comfort of your holy word,
we may embrace and for ever hold fast
the hope of everlasting life,
which you have given us in our Saviour Jesus Christ. Amen
(*Book of Common Prayer,* 2004)

Prayer of Humble Access

We do not presume
to come to this thy Table, O merciful Lord,
trusting in our own righteousness,
but in thy manifold and great mercies.
We are not worthy
so much as to gather up the crumbs under thy Table.
But thou art the same Lord,
whose property is always to have mercy:
Grant us therefore, gracious Lord,
so to eat the flesh of thy dear Son Jesus Christ,
 and to drink his blood,
 that our sinful bodies may be made clean by his body,
and our souls washed through his most precious blood,
 and that we may evermore dwell in him,
 and he in us. Amen.
(*Book of Common Prayer,* 2004)

Prayer before Sharing Bread and Wine

Come to this sacred table,
Not because you must but because you may;
Come, not to declare that you are righteous,
But that you desire to be true disciples of our Lord Jesus Christ;

Come, not because you are strong,
But because you are weak;
Not because you have any claims on heaven's rewards,
But because in your frailty and sin
You stand in constant need of heaven's mercy and help. Amen
from the service of Holy Communion for Lent and Passiontide,
(*Methodist Worship Book*, 1999)

A Prayer of St Chrysostom

Almighty God, you have given us grace at this time with one
accord to make our common supplication to you; and you have
promised through your well-beloved Son that when two or
three are gathered together in his Name you will be in the midst
of them: Fulfill now, O Lord, our desires and petitions as may
be best for us; granting us in this world knowledge of your
truth, and in the age to come life everlasting. Amen
(*Book of Common Prayer*, 2004)

A Prayer of the Eastern Church

Be mindful, O Lord,
of thy people present here before thee,
and of those who are absent through age,
sickness, or infirmity.
Care for the infants, guide the young,
support the aged, encourage the faint-hearted,
Collect the scattered,
and bring back the wandering to thy fold.
Travel with the voyagers, defend the widows,
shield the orphans, deliver the captives,
heal the sick.
Succour all who are in tribulation, necessity, or distress.
Remember for good all those that love us, and those that hate us,
and those that have desired us, unworthy as we are, to pray for them.
And those whom we have forgotten,
do thou, O Lord, remember.
For thou art the helper of the helpless,
the saviour of the lost,

the refuge of the wanderer, the healer of the sick.
Thou, who knowest the need of each one,
and hast heard their prayer,
grant unto each according to thy merciful loving-kindness,
and thy eternal love;
through Jesus Christ our Lord.
Amen
(*Book of Common Prayer*, 2004)

Collect for Peace (traditional and modern texts)

O God, who art the author of peace and lover of concord,
in knowledge of whom standeth our eternal life, whose service
is perfect freedom;
Defend us thy humble servants in all assaults of our enemies;
that we, surely trusting in thy defence,
 may not fear the power of any adversaries;
through the might of Jesus Christ our Lord. **Amen.**

O God, the author of peace and lover of concord,
to know you is eternal life, and to serve you is perfect freedom;
Defend us in all assaults of our enemies,
that we, surely trusting in your protection,
may not fear the power of any adversaries;
through Jesus Christ our Lord. **Amen.**

Collect for Grace (traditional and modern texts)

O Lord, our heavenly Father, almighty and everlasting God,
who hast safely brought us to the beginning of this day:
Defend us in the same with thy mighty power;
and grant that this day we fall into no sin,
neither run into any kind of danger;
but that all our doings may be ordered by thy governance,
to do always that is righteous in thy sight;
through Jesus Christ our Lord. **Amen**

O Lord, our heavenly Father, almighty and everliving God,
we give you thanks for bringing us safely to this day:
Keep us from falling into sin or running into danger,
and in all things guide us to know and do your will;
through Jesus Christ our Lord. **Amen.**

Collect at Holy Communion

(traditional and modern texts)

Prevent us, O Lord, in all our doings
with thy most gracious favour,
and further us with thy continual help;
That in all our works, begun, continued, and ended in thee,
We may glorify thy holy Name.
And finally by thy mercy obtain everlasting life;
Through Jesus Christ our Lord. **Amen**

Go before us, Lord, in all our doings,
with your most gracious favour,
and further us with your continual help;
that in all our works begun, continued and ended in you,
we may glorify your holy name,
and finally by your mercy attain everlasting life;
through Jesus Christ our Lord. **Amen**.

Evening Collect

Lighten our darkness, we beseech thee, O Lord;
and by thy great mercy
defend us from all perils and dangers of this night;
for the love of thy only Son, our Saviour Jesus Christ.
Amen.

(Book of Common Prayer, 2004)

24

4
Praying with the Wesleys

By Dudley Levistone Cooney

FOR MANY YEARS THE METHODIST CHURCH has observed May 24th annually as *Wesley Day*, that being the date of John Wesley's spiritual experience in 1738, which was the prelude to his establishment of the Methodist societies. His brother Charles had had a similar experience three days previously. The book *Common Worship*, published by the Church of England in 2000, adds to the calendar a number of lesser festivals including the following:

May 24: John and Charles Wesley, Evangelists, Hymn Writers, 1791 and 1788

The dates are those of their respective deaths. No Collect is provided for this occasion, but *Methodist Worship*, authorised by the Methodist Conference and published in 1999 has this:

Almighty God,
You raised up your servants, John and Charles Wesley,
To proclaim anew the gift of redemption and the life of holiness.
Pour out your Spirit,
and revive your work among us;
that inspired by the same faith,
and upheld by the same grace in word and sacrament,
we and all your children may be made one in the unity of your Church on earth,
even as in heaven we are made one in you;
through Jesus Christ our Lord. Amen.

On Christmas Day in 1747, John Wesley urged the Methodist people for the first time to renew their Covenant with God, following the biblical tradition.

In the French Church at Spitalfields in London on 11 August 1755 he held their first formal Covenant Service, using words from the English Puritans, Joseph and Richard Alleine. This Service, followed immediately by the administration of the Holy Communion, has became a regular observance on the first Sunday of a new year.

Some people have found Wesley's words too demanding, and have been reluctant to repeat them, but the prayer simply puts into words what is essentially the commitment of the Christian, whether explicit or implicit. Below we have placed the traditional version followed by the modern version from *Methodist Worship*:

Traditional

I am no longer my own, but Thine. Put me to what Thou wilt, rank me with whom Thou wilt; put me to doing, put me to suffering; let me be employed for Thee or laid aside for Thee; exalted for Thee or brought low for Thee; let me be full, let me be empty; let me have all things, let me have nothing; I freely and heartily yield all things to Thy pleasure and disposal.

And now, O glorious and blessed God, Father, Son and Holy Spirit, Thou art mine and I m Thine. So be it. And the Covenant which I have made on earth, let it be ratified in heaven. Amen.

Modern

I am no longer my own but yours.
Your will, not mine be done in all things,
wherever you may place me,
in all that I do
and in all that I may endure;
when there is work for me
and when there is none;
when I am troubled
and when I am at peace.

Your will be done
when I am valued
and when I am disregarded;
when I find fulfilment
and when it is lacking;
when I have all things
and when I have nothing.
I willingly offer
all that I have and am
to serve you
as and where you choose
Glorious and blessed God,
Father, Son and Holy Spirit
you are mine and I am yours.
May it be so for ever.
Let this covenant now made on earth
be fulfilled in heaven.   Amen

The prayer from the Covenant Service is careful to spell out the conditions and contrasts of daily living. In another context, John Wesley wrote the following prayer for forgiveness:

Forgive them all, O Lord:
our sins of omission and our sins of commission;
the sins of our youth and the sins of our riper years;
the sins of our souls and the sins of our bodies;
our secret and our more open sins;
our sins of ignorance and surprise,
and our more deliberate and presumptuous sins;
the sins we have done to please ourselves,
and the sins we have done to please others;
the sins we know and remember,
and the sins we have forgotten;
the sins we have striven to hide from others
and the sins by which we have offended others;
forgive them, O Lord, forgive them all for his sake,
who died for our sins and rose for our justification,
and now stands at your right hand to make intercession for us,
Jesus Christ our Lord.   Amen.

Behind this prayer lie the early Methodist disciplines of self-examination and mutual examination in small confidential bands. The way in which the prayer is phrased is a reminder that sin is not just wilful disobedience; rather it is anything that offends God. The Old Testament uses three words, one meaning missing the mark, another straying from the path, and the third disobeying a known command. That robs us of the defence 'We have done no harm!' and urges the question 'Have we done any good?' or in other words 'Have we been profitable servants?' (Luke 17:10). By contrast here is a prayer of John Wesley that runs to only a dozen words: ' O Lord, let us not live to be useless; for Christ's sake. Amen'.

With all its brevity it is a profound prayer. It again poses the question, 'What good have we done?' In debate with a Pharisee, Jesus underlined the two great commandments 'Love God and love your neighbour!' (Mark 12:28-34, Matthew 22:34-40). Usefulness lies in the practical expression we give to those.

The letter to the Church in Laodicea (Revelation 3:14-22) is the obvious inspiration behind another of John's prayers:

> Deliver me, Lord God, from a slothful mind, from all lukewarmness, and all dejection of spirit. I know these cannot but deaden my love for you; mercifully free my heart from them, and give me a lively, zealous, active and cheerful spirit; that I may vigorously whatever you command, thankfully suffer whatever you choose for me, and always be ardent to obey in all things your holy love. Amen

The word 'suffer' is now always associated with pain

or disaster, but it used to have the wider sense of accepting events or conditions. For example, in 'Suffer little children . . . to come unto me' (Matthew 19:14 King James version) it simply means 'permit', and in Wesley's prayer has the meaning 'accept'.

His use of the word 'cheerful' is also worth noting. It is not often used in the New Testament, but on two occasions (Romans 12:8 and 2 Corinthians 9:7) the Greek word behind it is the origin of the English 'hilarious'. The implication is an enthusiastic enjoyment. Christian faith and service are to be enjoyed!

The last of John Wesley's prayers to which we shall refer sets this enjoyment of faith and service in its context:

> You are never tired, O Lord, of doing us good; let us never be weary of doing you service. But as you have pleasure in the wellbeing of your servants, let us take pleasure in the service of our Lord, and abound in your work and in your love and praise evermore. Amen

Christian faith and service can be enjoyed when they are seen not as an imposed obligation, or as a means to an end, but as the outworking of a deep sense of gratitude to the God who has given so much more that we could ever deserve. It is giving thanks.

-o0o-

It need come as no surprise that the published prayers of Charles Wesley are all in verse. There is tendency to think of all his verses as hymns, but even his religious verses were not necessarily intended to be sung.

The Collection of Hymns for the People called Methodists (London, 1779) was as much a prayer book as a hymn book, being intended to inspire private prayer and meditation as well as provide for praise in public worship.

This prayer is one verse from the hymn 'Jesus, Lover of my soul' (*Hymns and Psalms* (hereafter H&P) 528, and the *Church Hymnal* (fifth edition) (hereafter CH) 53 which was first published in 1740. The inspiration for the first line of the hymn may have been the Apocryphal Book of Wisdom 11:26 'Thou sparest all, for they are Thine, O Lord, Thou Lover of souls'. Or it may have come from a similar reference in Thomas á Kempis, *The Imitation of Christ*, Book 3, Chapter 20 (1418):

Plenteous grace with thee is found,
Grace to cover all my sin;
Let the healing streams abound;
Make and keep me pure within.
Thou of life the fountain art,
Freely let me take of thee;
Spring thou up within my heart;
Rise to all eternity.

The idea of Jesus as a refuge in time of trouble may have appealed to the early Methodists suffering from varying degrees of persecution, but Charles sees the storms as inward, the storms of trial and temptation. He rejoices in the grace of God as the source of deliverance from sin, and of calm and strength in the times of need.

The hymn 'God of all power, and truth, and grace'

(HP 726) was first published in 1742 under the heading 'Pleading the promise of sanctification'. Among its 28 verses were these:

Purge me from every sinful blot,
My idols all be cast aside;
Cleanse me from every evil thought,
From all the filth of self and pride.

Give me a new, a perfect heart,
From doubt, and fear, and sorrow free;
The mind which was in Christ impart,
And let my spirit cleave to thee

John Wesley believed that God's chief purpose in calling the Methodists into existence was to spread scriptural holiness throughout the land. Holiness was not meant to be the achievement of the heroic few, but the fulfilment of every believer. In the verses below, Charles distinguishes the hindrances to that fulfilment – other things taking the place of God in the life of the individual such as selfishness, pride, doubt and adversity – and pleads for divine help in overcoming these. The scriptural inspiration of the hymn is Ezekiel 36:23-28. The hymn 'O thou who camest from above' (HP 745, CH 639) is a prayer in four verses:

O thou who camest from above,
The pure celestial fire to impart,
Kindle a flame of sacred love
On the mean altar of my heart.

There let it for thy glory burn
With inextinguishable blaze,
And trembling to its source return,
In humble prayer and fervent praise.

Jesus confirm my heart's desire
To work, and speak, and think for thee;
Still let me guard the holy fire,
And still stir up they gift in me –

Ready for all thy perfect will,
My acts of faith and love repeat,
Till death thy endless mercies seal,
And make the sacrifice complete.

The imagery in these verses is suggested by Leviticus 6:13. The hymn was first published in 1762, and there are allusions to at least nine other scriptural texts. The third verse echoes the old Collect for the 25th Sunday after Trinity – 'Stir up, we beseech thee, O Lord, the wills of thy faithful people. . .'. The new Collect for the 4th Sunday before Advent echoes Wesley – 'Almighty and everlasting God, who hast kindled the flame of love in the hearts of thy saints. . .'.

Christian faith, of course, is not just for Sundays. It must be taken into all the days of the week, and Charles helps us to pray for the business of the week in the following verses:

Forth in thy name, O Lord, I go,
My daily labour to pursue,
Thee, only thee, resolved to know
In all I think, or speak, or do.

The task thy wisdom hath assigned
O let me cheerfully fulfil,
In all my works thy presence find,
And prove thine acceptable will.

This hymn (HP 381, CH 567) was originally published

in 1749 with six verses, but more recently verse three is usually omitted. It is a prayer for grace to conduct all our affairs with integrity, and with concern for others. Other hymns reflect particular aspects of prevailing conditions in 18th-century Britain. For example, the hymns which Charles wrote for the coal miners at Kingswood, near Bristol, are never used now, but include such lines as the following which allude to the subterranean darkness in which the men worked:

For this, no longer sons of night,
To thee our thanks and hearts we give;
To thee who call'd us into light,
To thee we die, to thee we live.

Charles had a quite remarkable facility for finding language which fits the diverse situations of different people, thus reminding us of the relevance of faith to work in the context of his time.

Hymn books generally cater for public worship, and therefore contain little material on family life. Out of a total of 823 hymns, *Hymns & Psalms* has only 11 in the section headed 'Marriage and Family Life', out of 719 The Church Hymnal has only five for 'The Home and Family'. There could not be a place there for one of Charles's prayer hymns, published in 1767, in a small collection *Hymns for a Family*, and itself headed 'A father's prayer for his son'. But its opening verse deserves to be better known:

God of my thoughtless infancy,
My giddy youth and riper age,
Pierced with thy love, I worship thee,
My God, my guide through every stage;

From countless sins, and griefs, and snares
Preserved, thy guardian hand I own,
And borne and saved to hoary hairs,
Ask the same mercy for my son.

There is great charm in the way he contrasts his own youth and age, acknowledges the guidance of God in his won life, and prays the same for the next generation. In 1767 Charles had two sons, Charles Jun., then aged ten years, and Samuel, born the previous year who was just a year old. This verse alone opens a window on the intimacy of family prayer.

Of Charles's eight children, five died before they were a year old. That was not an uncommon experience in the 18th century, and godly parents sought to console themselves with the thought that their children were with God. The same small collection has 'A mother's act of resignation on the death of a child':

Child of prayer, by grace Divine
Him I willingly resign,
Through his last convulsive throes
Born into a true repose,
Born into the world above,
Glorious world of light and love!

The imagery is stark. Were the 'convulsive throes' those of baby John in 1753, and of whom nothing further is known? The point is that all the details of our agony in grief can be taken to God, whose heart is the heart of a perfect Father.

In the 1780s, as Charles approached his own old age, and a man in his 70s was older than a man of the same age now, he found the same hope in Jesus as he had done in 1738, when he was less than half as old. The phrase 'a helpless worm' may offend the squeamish taste of today, but it should not distract us from the fact that our Saviour is still, to borrow words from the hymn writer, Henry Francis Lyte, 'help of the helpless', and can help us to accept dependency:

In age and feebleness extreme,
Who shall a helpless worm redeem?
Jesus! My only hope thou art,
Strength of my failing flesh and heart;
O could I catch one smile from thee,
And drop into eternity

-o0o-

In 1956, the Epworth Press published a small volume *The Prayers of Susanna Wesley*. They had been drawn by the editor W. L. Doughty from meditations written by the mother of John and Charles Wesley. The youngest child of Dr Samuel Annesley, the leading Dissenting minister in London at the time, Susanna Annesley had been born in 1669. She was given a quite exceptional education for a woman of her time, reading Latin, Greek and French. In 1689, she married the Revd Samuel Wesley, a priest of the Church of England, and eight years later they moved to Epworth when he was appointed rector of that Lincolnshire parish. She and the rector had 19 children, of whom some ten survived to adult life. At the best of times required to manage on a small stipend, her husband was imprisoned for debt the care of the family devolved entirely on her. After her husband's death she lived with either John or Charles, and died at John's house in 1742. In spite of the pressures on her time, she preserved a short period each day for prayer and meditation, and it was during these that the meditations were written. None of them is dated, but a selection is reproduced here:

Help me, Lord, to remember that religion is not to be confined to the church or closet, nor exercised only in prayer and meditation, but that everywhere I am in thy presence. So may my every word and action have a moral content. As defects and infirmities betray themselves in the daily accidents and common conversations of like, grant me thy grace, O Lord, that I may watch over, regulate and govern them. Enable me so to know myself and those with whom I have to do, that I may conform to the precepts of the Gospel and train myself to those rules of wisdom and virtue of which I am capable. . . May all things instruct me and afford me an opportunity of exercising some virtue and daily learning and growing toward thy likeness, let the world go which way it will. Amen

Help me. O Lord, to make a true use of all disappointments and calamities in this life, in such wise that they may unite my heart more closely with thee. . . Until this temper of mind be attained I can never enjoy any settled peace, much less a calm serenity. Thou only, O God, canst satisfy my immortal soul and bestow those spiritual pleasures which alone are proper to its nature. . . Enable me to love thee, my God, with all my heart, with all my mind, with all my strength; so to love thee as to desire thee; so to desire thee as to be uneasy without Thee, without Thy favour, without some such resemblance to thee as my nature in this imperfect state can bear. Amen

Enable me, O God, to collect and compose my thoughts before an immediate approach to thee in prayer. May I be careful to have my mind in order when I take upon myself the honour to speak to the Sovereign Lord of the Universe, remembering that upon the temper of my soul depends, in very great measure, my success. Thou art infinitely too great to be trifled with; too wise to be imposed on by a mock devotion and dost abhor a sacrifice without a heart. Help me to entertain an habitual sense of thy perfections, as an admirable help against cold and formal performances. Save me from engaging in rash and precipitate prayers and from abrupt breaking away to follow business or pleasure, as though I had never prayed. Amen

I thank thee, O God, because I know that religion does not mean melancholy and moroseness, tending only to destroy the comforts of our environment. But I have learned that all things in the world, where religion is wanting, cannot possibly make men happy or easy to themselves or others. . . When I am peevish and morose, it is not because of religion, but of my want of it. Help me not to be discouraged by my own failures, nor to spend too much time in thinking on them, remembering that perfection is my Saviour's endowment and sincerity is mine. Help me with firm faith to rely on his merits, joined with my sincere endeavour to obey thy whole will. Amen

I praise thee, O God, for any ability to serve thee and for enabling me to perform relative duties, which are a great part of natural and revealed religion. I am apt to be discouraged by the constant sense of my infirmities, but thou, O God, wilt not despise the day of small things. It is thy grace that makes me what I am, that keeps me to stated times of devotion and that in any measure preserves me from total apostacy. I grant that my performances are mean and contemptible and unworthy of thine acceptance, yet, if thou didst utterly reject them, thou wouldest not so often give me grace to repent and enable me to rejoice in any little victory which I get over my daily infirmities. I would not willingly offend thee, and I therefore rely upon the merits of my Saviour and never despair of mercy. Amen

Let it be my great care, O God, to have special regard to justice and charity, to preserve the principles of faith inviolate, and in all cases to perform present duty with the greatest exactness and integrity. And whenever crosses or trouble are met without, may all be well within, and the consciousness of my own innocence be an admirable preservative against all exterior calamities! So grant that it may not be in the power of any to rob me of that peace which results in a firm trust in thee, through the merits of our blessed Saviour, to whom with thee and the Sacred Spirit, be all glory! Amen

Individually these prayers need little comment, but there are a number of features that deserve remark. These are the prayers of a woman with a remarkable degree of self-knowledge, who doesn't waste time making excuses for herself, but rather learns from her mistakes and lapses. At the present time, when the principle of the importance of the individual has strayed into the notion of self-importance, Susanna Wesley's humility is challenging. In this age when manners are generally more casual, and that casualness has crept into some worship, her deferential language, albeit old fashioned, is a valuable corrective. With all that there is an intimacy in the way in which she discusses her own character with the Almighty. The God who is the Other is also the Friend.

5

Wesley Hymns

Notes by Dudley Levistone Cooney

CHARLES WESLEY (1707-88) WAS A FOUNDER, with his elder brother John, of Methodism, and a priest of the Church of England. He was an exceptionally prolific writer of poetry, including a large number of hymns. He spent several months in Ireland in 1747 and in 1748.

His hymns had three purposes:

1. In common with all church music they expressed the worshipper's joy in Christian faith.

2. Those that were not sung in church were offered for reading in private devotion, where they would afford material for inspiration and meditation.

3. They were the means by which the Methodist people learned their faith; songs are more easily memorable than read or spoken words.

With a few exceptions, the hymns analysed below are common to the *Church Hymnal* (fifth edition) (**CH5**) and *Hymns & Psalms* (**H&P**).

The analysis here should be used in conjunction with the texts available in both sources. Hymn numbers in both are provided under the title of each hymn.

And can it be that I should gain . . .
CH5 218   **H&P** 216

Among evangelicals of all denominations this is possibly the most popular of Charles Wesley's hymns. It has been sung with great, and not always appropriate, gusto. The first verse is an expression of amazement that the singer has been redeemed by the grace of God – a gift not to be taken for granted. The verse should be sung with the bated breath of sheer wonder. CH5 omits the second of the verses in H&P and thus loses the thrill of the paradox of salvation: 'the Immortal dies!' The tone of astonishment continues to the dramatic expression of the sense of deliverance. In the final verse the note is one of assurance, thanks entirely to the grace of God in Christ, and the gusto becomes appropriate.

The hymn was written immediately after his evangelical conversion, and has an intimately personal flavour. Notable is the way in which one aspect of the Incarnation is condensed into a single line: 'Emptied himself of all but love'. The verse beginning 'Long my imprisoned spirit lay' compares the singer's experience to Peter's escape from prison (Acts 12: 6-7).

Christ the Lord is risen today
H&P 193
Love's redeeming work is done
CH5 277

These are not two different hymns, but selected verses from one original that had no less than 11. One of the greatest hymns expressing the joy of the resurrection, it has been much altered by later editors. Traditionally it was sung on Easter Sunday, but the *Methodist Alternative Form for Holy Communion* (1936) placed some lines of it as a thanksgiving for the sacrament, and the current *Methodist Worship* now gives it the same place in the first form of service for ordinary seasons. By omitting the first verse CH5 makes it more readily useable throughout the year. Every Sunday is a celebration of the Resurrection – 'a little Easter Day'.

Christ whose glory fills the skies
CH5 52   **H&P** 457

Apart from its value as a hymn, this is a poem of very high quality. Originally published in 1740 under the title 'A Morning Hymn', it is more a celebration of the light of Christ's presence. The idea of the Messiah coming like a sunrise is quite common in Old Testament prophesy (eg Malachi 4:2). Charles Wesley turns it into a prayer for personal enlightenment, and goes further. By his likening sin to gloom, he makes it also a prayer for holiness. The language reflects the closing words of the Benedictus (Luke 1:78, 79) in the *Book of Common Prayer* (2004) p.122.

Come thou long expected Jesus
CH5 119   **H&P** 81

This hymn first appeared in *Hymns for the Nativity of our Lord*, published in 1744. It does not specifically look to Christ's coming in glory. Rather it invites the Christ who has already come in to the world to enter the hearts of the worshippers who are singing. In simple, but graphic language it expresses the central ideas of Christian faith – deliverance, hope, joy and the rule of God in our hearts – and affirms our dependence on the merits of our Saviour. The Christ of this hymn is the Christ who, by his Spirit, is involved in the life of the believer and leads the believer to the fulfilment of his/her faith in the kingdom of God.

Forth in thy name, O Lord, I go
CH5 567   **H&P** 381

This hymn originally had six verses. Wesley's third verse which is now omitted read as follows:

> Preserve me from my calling's snare,
> And hide my simple heart above,
> Above the thorns of choking care,
> The gilded baits of worldly love.

Such language was considered too strong for the 19th and 20th centuries in which religion was not allowed to interfere with economic ambition, and thus left out, while the second verse in line four has been altered from: 'And prove thine acceptable will'. The present version is easier to sing, but loses the reference to Romans 12:2. Verse four line one follows Matthew 11:30 'My yoke is easy and my burden is light'. The yoke was a piece of timber that linked two oxen to the plough, and an 'easy' yoke was one which fitted the animals so well that their necks were not galled. The carpenter of Nazareth would have known how to make such yokes.

This is one of the very few hymns which clearly recognises the routine of daily work as the arena in which most Christians work out their vocation.

Hail the day that sees him rise
CH5 266   **H&P** 197

This hymn for Ascension-tide originally consisted of ten verses. CH5 retains seven of these whilst H&P has six, but the latter makes more radical alterations. The original second line: 'Ravished from our wishful eyes' suggests the reluctance of the believer to lose sight of the Saviour, and this is counteracted in the following verses. In them the hymn reassures us that Christ triumphantly returning to his native heaven, still bears the signs of his humanity and cares for humankind. In the 18th century, the word 'ravish' meant 'take from life or from sight'; its change of meaning justifies its removal in the CH5 version. The Alleluias at the end of each line were added in 1852.

In CH5, the first five verses and in H&P the four follow the sequence of the Ascension. The last two verses in each book change from narrative to prayer that the worshippers may participate in this. They relate to the Collect for the Day.

Hark! The herald-angels sing
CH5 160   **H&P** 106

This well-loved Christmas hymn was first published (1739) with ten four-line verses, the last four of which are never now used. St Patrick's Cathedral in Dublin preserves four-line tradition, but with the first two lines repeated as a refrain. The present form of three eight-line verses with the first two lines as a refrain dates from *Wesley's Hymns* (1877) when it was made to fit the present tune *Mendelssohn*. The first two lines originally read:

> 'Hark, how all the welkin rings
> Glory to the King of kings. . .(refrain)'

The word 'welkin' for the vault of heaven was already going out of use, and the lines were given their present form by George Whitefield in 1753. The last two lines retain their original form in H&P, but have been given a genderinclusive form in CH5:

> 'born to raise each child of earth,
> born to give us second birth'.

The hymn is like a diamond abounding with biblical references, and describing the many facets of the incarnation.

Jesu, lover of my soul
CH5   553   H&P 528

Unlike his brother Charles, John Wesley was always reluctant to use terms of endearment in relation to God, and this may be the reason why this hymn did not get into the *Collection of Hymns For the Use of the People Called Methodists* until the 1797 edition, six years after John's death. Others have found difficulty with the line 'while the nearer waters roll'. Julian's *Dictionary of Hymnology*, however, makes the point that storms at sea can be very local, and on his first journey to Ireland in 1747, John Wesley notes in his *Journal* that a fresh gale drove the ship on which he was travelling, while another ship a mile away lay becalmed.

The hymn was first published in 1740 under the title 'In temptation'. This makes it clear that it is intended for times of particular stress, and is not intended to encourage a flight from the harsh realities of life. In the years when Methodists suffered persecution in England and Ireland this hymn must have had deep meaning for them. In the five verses there are more than 20 scriptural allusions. In the last verse water, which has been threat up to this, is used as the metaphor of spiritual life. That the trial can become a source of grace is not an unusual hindsight.

Jesus, the name high over all
CH5 99   **H&P** 264

The original text of this hymn was a poem of 22 verses. It remains one of the great hymns of praise declaring the sovereignty of Jesus over the universe, and has been frequently used on occasions of exorcism. The power of the name of Jesus should not be understood as a magical incantation. In the Bible the name of a person represented his or her nature, which is why there are instances of a change of name following a change of character. It is the nature of Jesus – who and what he is – that is the source of power.

The last three verses of the hymn are another expression of the conviction that God's grace – his power to change – is available to every human being: man, woman and child. It therefore becomes a priority for the believer to ensure that as many people as possible know this, and the singing of these lines is an act of commitment to spreading the news.

Lo, he comes with clouds descending
CH5 132   **H&P** 241

This splendid acclamation of Christ's coming in glory, rich in scriptural language, has had a chequered history with versions attributed to John Cennick and Martin Madan, and with many different later alterations. The words in H&P follow Charles Wesley's original; those in CH5 incorporate the work of John Cennick, who had been a Methodist, became a Moravian, and founded the Moravian Church in Ireland.

The tune, now called *Helmsley*, was originally called *Olivers*, and was said to have been adapted by Thomas Olivers from a tune he had heard whistled in the street. There is, however, no certainty about this. Hymn and tune have been linked since 1765.

The original lines (altered in CH5) have been seen by some as anti-Semitic:

'Those who set at nought and sold him,
Pierced and nailed him to the tree'…

This seems to be over sensitive, as the piercing and nailing were certainly done by Gentiles. The CH5 change from 'those' to 'we' does more than avoid this question. More importantly it reminds us as human beings that *we* were represented at the Cross by those who carried out the crucifixion.

Love divine, all loves excelling
CH5 634   **H&P** 267

Charles Wesley's idea for this hymn was derived from a song by Dryden in Purcell's opera *King Arthur*, 'Fairest isle, all isles excelling'. Charles wrote an amount of secular verse in the style of Dryden, and at least one critic has argued that some of this work should have been included in the great anthologies of English verse. The second line, 'Joy of heaven to earth come down' is not a prayer; it is faith's description of the divine love.

Each of the verses makes a different prayer. The first prays that Christ will enter every heart. The second asks that we may all know his life within us. The third begs that we may be made ready for the transforming glory of heaven.

Verse three line two originally read 'Pure and sinless let us be'. Given the Wesleyan doctrine of holiness the modern version is unfortunately weak. Achievement generally falls short of the ideal, but if you lower the ideal you also lower the measure of achievement. Donald English made the point that the remarkable fact about the early Methodists was not that they became holy, but that they made a serious effort towards it.

O for a heart to praise my God
CH5 638   **H&P** 536

The text of this hymn was based on Psalm 51:10, 'Create in me a clean heart, O God, and renew a right spirit within me'. CH5 places this hymn in the section on 'Holiness'; H&P in the section on 'Confession and Supplication'. Originally of eight verses, verses five to seven are nowadays usually omitted. The Companion to H&P adds six other scriptural references, and reminds us that one is from Ephesians 3:14-19, one of Charles Wesley's most often used texts.

CH5 retains Charles Wesley's original line 'My dear Redeemer's praise' while H&P follows John Wesley's emendation 'My great Redeemer's praise'. Both books use John's 'gracious Lord' in verse five rather than the original 'dearest Lord'. Charles was quite happy to express his emotions; John was more cautious, and was particularly wary of being over familiar with the Almighty. This was a danger that later revivalists were less successful in avoiding.

The clean heart for which the Psalmist prays is now seen as one that has been cleansed by the atoning death of Christ, in which the Redeemer is king, and in which every thought is new. This last reflects the fact that, while we think of the heart as the seat of the emotions, the Old Testament writers viewed it as the organ of thought. In any case, the hymn is a prayer for the renewal of the whole personality.

O for a thousand tongues to sing
CH5 104   **H&P** 744

In conversation with Charles, the Moravian pastor in London Peter Böhler said: 'Had I a thousand tongues I would praise Him with them all'. The idea became the first line of the hymn as we now know it. In 1739

John and Charles Wesley began the work from which the Methodist Church developed, and 'O for a thousand tongues to sing' was published in the following year, making it one of the earliest Methodist hymns. From 1780 to 1983 it was always the first hymn in the Wesleyan Methodist hymnbooks, and has never lost its popularity. The original hymn had 18 verses and began with the line 'Glory to God, and praise and love'. The H&P version of eight verses comprises those numbered seven to 12, 14-18 in the original, and abridgement dating from 1753; CH5 uses only seven to 12, and transposes verse eight to the end.

ICH5 preserves Charles's original second line, 'My dear Redeemer's praise'; H&P prefers John's emendation, 'My great Redeemer's praise' (See 553, 528 and 638, 536 above).

Surprisingly the *Methodist Hymn Book* (1933) omitted the verse which begins 'Hear him ye deaf, his praise ye dumb', depriving worshippers of an exciting reference to the Gospel miracles. The first two lines of verse three (CH5), verse four (H&P) have been seen as indicating the two-fold character of the Atonement (cf 'Rock of Ages. . . cleanse me from its guilt and power). It is an exuberant acclamation of the saving work of Christ.

O love divine what has thou done
CH5 234   **H&P** 175

The dependence of this hymn on the text of Lamentations 1:12 is rather lost in H&P by the omission of verse two, which CH5 retains. However, CH5 does amend the third line of the verse from Charles Wesley's original: 'Come see, ye worms, your Maker die'. The graphic contrast between the immensity of salvation and the little we have made of ourselves is just too much for modern sensibilities. The hymn is a powerful expression of the wonder of the believer that Christ's redeeming love should reach to him or her as an individual. Verse two balances that in a particularly forceful way by the inclusion of 'all ye that pass by', a balance that is always present to Charles Wesley's mind. Without it the 'all' of verses three and four is in danger of being interpreted too narrowly. In their *Companion to the Church Hymnal*, Darling and Davison comment that this hymn is a particularly suitable choice for the three hours devotion on Good Friday.

O thou who camest from above
CH5 639   **H&P** 745

The basis of this hymn is Leviticus 6:13 which includes the text: 'the fire must be kept burning continuously', but Charles Wesley moves the altar from the Temple to the human heart, and the High Priest who kindles the fire is Christ. In their *Works of John Wesley*, editors Hildebrandt and Beckerlegge identify no fewer than 22 scripture texts behind these 16 lines. Always now printed as four verses of four lines, the hymn was originally in two verses of eight lines. If the present verses three and four are read as one verse, it helps to clarify the meaning of the whole without altering the original wording.

This superb hymn is a perfect description of 'inward'

as opposed to formal religion. It makes clear that faith is the gift of Christ, and prays for his assistance in keeping it alive and active. The hymn is set to the tune *Hereford* in CH5, and this is also the first set tune in H&P. It was composed by Samuel Sebastian Wesley, a grandson of Charles.

Peace be to this congregation
CH5 505

This little known hymn first appeared in the second volume of Wesley's *Hymns and Sacred Poems* (1749) where the first line is 'Peace be to this habitation'. It then had six verses of eight lines. The present first line has been traced back to some of the earlier editions of Lady Huntingdon's *Collection of Hymns* (cf. Darling and Davison). It seems to have disappeared from English and Irish usage, but was included in a number of American books.

It was used at the annual conference of the Hymn Society of Great Britain when it met at Bangor in North Wales in 1990, and it was this use that led to the hymn's inclusion in CH5.

The three verses therein provided are a delightful commentary on the peace of God, and it has been suggested that it would be very appropriate to the exchange of peace in the Holy Communion office. It offers a defence against an understanding of fellowship which reduces it to 'socialising'.

Rejoice, the Lord is King
CH5 281   **H&P** 243

This superbly crafted hymn first appeared in 1746 in a small collection under the title *Hymns For Our Lord's Resurrection*. CH5 includes it in the section for 'His resurrection and ascension'. H&P has it under 'Christ's coming in glory'. The heading under which it appears is not important, for it remains a glorious celebration of Christ's victory over evil and death.

The original fifth verse was retained in the *Methodist Hymn Book* of 1933, but was dropped at the publication of the present edition in 1983. It read:

> He all his foes shall quell,
> Shall all our sins destroy,
> And every bosom swell
> With pure seraphic joy.

The refrain to the first four verses combines the exhortation in the Holy Communion Office with that in Philippians 4:4, and the final refrain draws on the text of I Corinthians 15:52. The succession of the verses follows that of the relevant articles in the Apostle's Creed. What Charles Wesley is doing is drawing out the thrill that those articles contain, and that is at the heart of our faith.

The tune *Gopsal*, now inseparably linked to this hymn, was written for it by Handel, but apparently lost for some 70 years until 1826, when the manuscript was rediscovered by Charles Wesley's son Samuel in the library of the Fitzwilliam Museum in Cambridge.

Soldiers of Christ arise
CH5 487   **H&P** 719

CH5 simply offers three verses of eight lines for this hymn. H&P complicates it by printing two parts, with a total of 14 verses of four lines, but numbered as seven to fit the tune by Naylor which is favoured in both books. It originally appeared in 1742 appended to John Wesley's tract: *The Character of a Methodist*, where it had 16 verses of eight lines each.

The hymn is an expansion of the text of Ephesians 6:13-18: 'the whole armour of God'. To call it a meditation or even a commentary would be misleading. The metre of the hymn, double short metre, has a lively beat which suggests the tramp of marching feet, and one commentator has called this Charles Wesley's 'fighting metre'. It demands that the singer be ready for active service in the cause of Christ.

Son of God, if thy free grace
        H&P 720

This is a very fine expression of the Methodist emphasis on the need for continued faith to final salvation. The God who redeems is the one who keeps the redeemed by his grace. The means of that grace are the sacrament, public worship, Bible reading, fellowship and private prayer. Those who neglect these put themselves in danger of losing the grace which they mediate. The tune *Gersau*, set in H&P, is hauntingly beautiful and underscores the lines superbly.

Thou God of truth and love
H&P 374

This hymn originated as a love poem which Charles wrote for his bride-to-be, Sally Gwynne, shortly before their wedding, and may have been first used on that occasion. In the original lines:

> That both might one remain (verse 3 line 2)
> Till both thine utmost goodness prove (verse 3 line 5)
> Till both receive the starry crown (verse 4 line 6)

The word 'both' was altered in 1749 by John Wesley to 'we' and 'all' and 'all' in each case to enable the hymn to be used congregationally. Many couples have found the hymn, even as altered, inspirational at their own weddings. As hymns are then usually printed in full on orders of service, its absence from CH5 would not be a barrier to its use by others.

Ye servants of God, your Master proclaim
CH5 492   H&P 278

This hymn owes its principal inspiration to Psalm 147 and Revelation 7:9-12. Other scriptural texts are reflected in it. In fact, Wesley's hymns are full of such allusions. It was not that Charles sat down with a Bible and a concordance to look for texts to support what he was writing. He and his brother John had so studied the Bible that its language permeated their thinking, and it came to them naturally when they thought of aspects of the faith.

The hymn was written in 1744, at a time of political insecurity in England, when the Methodists as a new group were under attack, and the Wesleys were accused of being Jesuits and Jacobites. The omission of the original verses two and three has created the happy pattern in which the closing line of each verse is echoed in the opening line of the next.

It is a call to adoration and praise, and also to the proclamation of the redeeming grace of God.

JOHN WESLEY (1703 -91) WITH HIS YOUNGER BROTHER
Charles, was a founder of Methodism, and a priest of
the Church of England. He continued to direct the
Methodist societies throughout his life. He made 21
visits to Ireland between 1747 and 1789.

Jesus, thy blood and righteousness
CH5 671   **H&P** 225

Nicolaus von Zinzendorf was the leader of the
Moravian Brethren at Herrnhut in Germany. In 1738,
the Wesleys came under the influence of groups of
Moravians in Georgia and London, but parted from
them in 1739 when the English Moravians adopted a
position of quietism. Zinzendorf's hymn had 33 verses, of which John Wesley translated some 24. CH5 and
H&P have made different selections from these.

The importance of this hymn lies in its assertion of
the total dependence of the believer on the grace of
God, one of the central doctrines of the Reformation.
The H&P version makes this a fully personal confession of faith; CH5 chooses to end on a note that
brings in all of humanity.

Notes for this chapter:

- There are three Charles Wesley hymns in CH5 not in H&P, and 137 in H&P not in CH5. We have noted one of the former and two of the latter.

- Words should be checked before using the two hymnals simultaneously in joint congregations as editors have made different alterations.

Sources:

E. Darling & D. Davison, *Companion to the Church Hymnal* (Dublin, 2005)

F. Hildebrandt & O. A.Beckerlegge, *The Works of John Wesley* Volume 7: *A Collection of Hymns* (Oxford, 1983)

R. Watson & K. Trickett, *Companion to Hymns & Psalms* (Peterborough, 1988)

6

The Covenant Service

THE GATHERING OF THE PEOPLE OF GOD

HYMN

Let us pray:

> Glory to the Father, the God of love,
> who created us;
> who continually preserves and sustains us;
> who has loved us with an everlasting love,
> and given us the light of the knowledge of his
> glory
> in the face of Jesus Christ.

Blessèd be God for ever.

> Glory to Jesus Christ our Saviour,
> who, though he was rich,
> yet for our sake became poor,
> and was tested in every way as we are,
> yet without sin;
> who proclaimed the good news of the kingdom,
> and was obedient to the point of death,
> even death on a cross;
> who was raised from the dead and is alive for ever,
> and has opened the kingdom of heaven
> to all who trust in him;
> who is seated at God's right hand in glory,
> and will come to be our judge.

Blessèd be God for ever.

Glory to the Holy Spirit,
the Lord, the giver of life,
by whom we are born into the family of God,
and made members of the body of Christ;
whose witness confirms us;
whose wisdom teaches us;
whose power enables us;
who will do for us more than we can ask or
think.

Blessèd be God for ever.

To the one God, Father, Son and Holy Spirit,
be praise and glory for ever. **Amen.**

Silence

God of grace,
through the mediation of your Son,
you call us into a new covenant.
Help us therefore to draw near with faith
and join ourselves in a perpetual covenant with you;
through Jesus Christ our Lord. **Amen.**

THE MINISTRY OF THE WORD

A reading from the Law: *Exodus 24:3-11*
For the wisdom that guides us
we praise you, O God.

A reading from the Prophets: *Jeremiah 31:31-34*
For the word that inspires us
we praise you, O God.

A reading from the Epistles: *Romans 12:1-2*

For the truth that enlightens us
we praise you, O God.

GOSPEL READING

A reading from the Gospel according to . . .

Hear the Gospel of Christ.
Glory to Christ our Saviour.

This is the Gospel of Christ.
Praise to Christ our Lord.

SERMON

HYMN

THE COVENANT

GOD MADE A COVENANT with the people of Israel, calling them to be a holy nation, chosen to bear witness to his steadfast love by finding delight in the law.

The covenant was renewed in Jesus Christ our Lord, in his life, work, death and resurrection. In him all people may be set free from sin and its power, and united in love and obedience.

In this covenant God promises us new life in Christ. For our part we promise to live no longer for ourselves but for God.

We meet, therefore, as generations have met before us, to renew the covenant which bound them and binds us to God.

Let us then seek forgiveness for the sin by which we have denied God's claim upon us.

Let us pray:
> God of mercy, hear us as we confess our sins.
> For the sin that has made us slow to learn from
> Christ,
> reluctant to follow him,
> and afraid to bear the cross:
>
> Lord, have mercy,
> **Lord, forgive.**
>
> For the sin that has caused the poverty of our
> worship,
> the formality and selfishness of our prayers,
> our neglect of fellowship and the means of grace,
> and our hesitating witness for Christ:
>
> Lord, have mercy,
> **Lord, forgive.**
>
> For the sin that has led us to misuse your gifts,
> evade our responsibilities,
> and fail to be good stewards of your creation:
>
> Lord, have mercy,
> **Lord, forgive.**
>
> For the sin that has made us unwilling to over-
> come evil with good,
> tolerant of injustice,
> quick to condemn,
> and selfish in sharing your love with others:

Lord, have mercy,
Lord, forgive.

Silence

**Have mercy on me, O God,
in your constant love;
in the fullness of your mercy
blot out my offences.
Wash away all my guilt,
and cleanse me from my sin.
Create in me a clean heart, O God,
and renew a right spirit within me.
Give me the joy of your help again
and strengthen me with a willing spirit.**

The presiding minister says:
If we confess our sins,
God is faithful and just,
and will forgive our sins,
and cleanse us from all unrighteousness.

Therefore to all who truly repent
this is his gracious word:
'Your sins are forgiven'.
Amen. Thanks be to God.

HYMN

**Come, let us use the grace divine,
And all, with one accord,
In a perpetual cov'nant join
Ourselves to Christ the Lord:**

Give up ourselves, through Jesu's power,
His name to glorify;
And promise, in this sacred hour,
For God to live and die.
The cov'nant we this moment make
Be ever kept in mind:
We will no more our God forsake,
Or cast his words behind.

We never will throw off his fear
Who hears our solemn vow;
And if thou art well pleased to hear,
Come down, and meet us now.

To each the cov'nant blood apply,
Which takes our sins away;
And register our names on high,
And keep us to that day.

The people remain standing and the presiding minister says:

Sisters and brothers in Christ,
let us again accept our place within this covenant
which God has made with us and with all who are
called to be Christ's disciples.

This means that, by the help of the Holy Spirit,
we accept God's purpose for us,
and the call to love and serve God
in all our life and work.

Christ has many services to be done:
some are easy, others are difficult;
some bring honour, others bring reproach;
some are suitable to our natural inclinations and
material interests,

others are contrary to both;
in some we may please Christ and please ourselves;
in others we cannot please Christ except by denying
ourselves.
Yet the power to do all these things is given to us in
Christ, who strengthens us.

Therefore let us make this covenant of God our
own.
Let us give ourselves to him,
trusting in his promises and relying on his grace.

Eternal God,
in your faithful and enduring love
you call us to share in your gracious covenant in
Jesus Christ.
In obedience we hear and accept your commands;
in love we seek to do your perfect will;
with joy we offer ourselves anew to you.
We are no longer our own but yours.

I am no longer my own but yours.
Your will, not mine, be done in all things,
wherever you may place me,
in all that I do
and in all that I may endure;
when there is work for me
and when there is none;
when I am troubled
and when I am at peace.
Your will be done
when I am valued
and when I am disregarded;
when I find fulfilment
and when it is lacking;
when I have all things,
and when I have nothing.

I willingly offer
all I have and am
to serve you,
as and where you choose.

Glorious and blessèd God,
Father, Son and Holy Spirit,
you are mine and I am yours.
May it be so for ever.
Let this covenant now made on earth
be fulfilled in heaven. Amen.

Silence, all seated

As we have entered this covenant not for ourselves
alone, but as God's servants and witnesses, let us
pray for the Church and for the world.

Loving God, hear us as we pray for your holy catholic
Church:
make us all one, that the world may believe.

Inspire and lead all who govern and hold authority in
the nations of the world:
establish justice and peace among all people.

Have compassion on all who suffer from any sickness, grief or trouble:
deliver them from their distress.

We praise you for all your saints who have entered
your eternal glory:
bring us all to share in your heavenly kingdom.

Let us pray in silence for our own needs and for
those of others . . .

Silence

Lord our God,
you have helped us by your grace
to make these prayers,
and you have promised through Christ our Lord
that when two or three agree in his name
you will grant what they ask.
Answer now your servants' prayers
according to their needs;
in this world grant that we may truly know you,
and in the world to come
graciously give us eternal life;
through Jesus Christ our Lord. **Amen.**

THE LORD'S SUPPER

All stand

The Peace:
The Lord has made an everlasting covenant of peace
with his people.

The peace of the Lord be always with you.
And also with you.

The people may greet one another in the name of Christ.

THE PREPARATION OF THE GIFTS

HYMN

*The offerings of the people are presented. Bread and wine are
brought to the table (or if already on the table are uncovered).*

The presiding minister takes the bread and wine and prepares them for use.

THE THANKSGIVING

All stand

The presiding minister leads the great prayer of thanksgiving:

The Lord be with you.
And also with you.

Lift up your hearts.
We lift them to the Lord.

Let us give thanks to the Lord our God.
It is right to give our thanks and praise.

God our Father, fountain of goodness,
creator of all that is,
you have made us in your own image.
You have given us life and reason,
and love for one another,
setting in our hearts a hunger for you.

In darkness you are our light,
in adversity and temptation our strength.
You bear patiently with our folly and sin,
granting us your law to guide us
and your prophets to renew our faith.

In the fullness of time
you came to us in love and mercy
in Jesus Christ, your living Word,
full of grace and truth.

He lived among us,
declaring your forgiveness
and revealing your wisdom
in works of mercy and in his word of power.
For us he suffered and died upon the cross,
by death destroying death.
You raised him from the dead
and exalted him to your right hand on high.
Through him you sent your Holy Spirit
to be the life and light of your people,
gathered together in every time and place
to glorify your holy name.

With them and all the company of heaven
we join in the unending hymn of praise:

Holy, holy, holy Lord,
God of power and might,
heaven and earth are full of your glory.
Hosanna in the highest.
Blessèd is he who comes in the name of the
Lord.
Hosanna in the highest.

Holy God, pour out your Spirit
that these gifts of bread and wine
may be for us the body and blood
of your Son Jesus Christ our Lord,
who, on the night in which he was betrayed,
took bread, gave thanks, broke it,
and gave it to his disciples, saying,
'Take this and eat it.
This is my body given for you.
Do this in remembrance of me.'

In the same way, after supper,
he took the cup, gave thanks,
and gave it to them, saying,
'Drink from it, all of you.
This is my blood of the new covenant,
poured out for you and for many,
for the forgiveness of sins.
Do this, whenever you drink it,
in remembrance of me.'

Christ has died.
Christ is risen.
Christ will come again.

And so, Lord, we obey his command
with this bread and this cup,
by which we recall his death and resurrection,
the source of our life and salvation.
Grant that we, who share in this holy sacrament,
may be united by your Spirit
and grow into perfect love.

Bring us,
with those who have done your will in every age,
into the light of your presence
and the joy of your kingdom.

Through Christ, with Christ, in Christ,
in the power of the Holy Spirit,
we worship you in songs of everlasting praise.
Blessing and honour and glory and power
be yours for ever and ever. Amen.

The Lord's Prayer

We say together the prayer that Jesus gave us:

Our Father in heaven,
hallowed be your Name,
your kingdom come,
your will be done,
on earth as in heaven.
Give us today our daily bread.
Forgive us our sins
as we forgive those who sin against us.
Save us from the time of trial
and deliver us from evil.
For the kingdom, the power and the glory are
yours,
now and for ever. Amen.

The Breaking of the Bread

The presiding minister breaks the bread in the sight of the
people in silence, or saying:

The things of God for God's holy people.

Jesus Christ is holy;
Jesus Christ is Lord.
Glory to God the Father.

Silence, all seated or kneeling

The Sharing of the Bread and Wine

The presiding minister, those assisting with the distribution,
and the people receive, according to local custom.

The presiding minister may invite the congregation to receive
communion with these or similar words:

Jesus said: 'I am the bread of life.
Those who come to me shall not hunger
and those who believe in me shall never thirst.'

Draw near with faith.

Words such as the following are said during the distribution:

The body of Christ keep you in eternal life.
Amen.

The blood of Christ keep you in eternal life.
Amen.

During the distribution there may be appropriate music.

The elements that remain are covered with a white cloth.

PRAYERS AND DISMISSAL

Silence

Let us pray.
**Faithful God,
with these holy gifts
you have fed and strengthened us
in Jesus Christ your Son.
Guide us on our way,
that with all your faithful people
we may come to share the feast
of your eternal kingdom;
through Jesus Christ our Lord. Amen.**

HYMN

The presiding minister says:

The blessing of God,
the Father, the Son and the Holy Spirit,
be upon *you/us* and remain with *you/us* for ever.
Amen.

The presiding minister says:

Go in peace to love and serve the Lord.

In the name of Christ. Amen.

COVENANT

between

the Methodist Church in Ireland
and the Church of Ireland

1. We acknowledge one another's Churches as belonging to the One, Holy, Catholic and Apostolic Church of Jesus Christ, and as truly participating in the apostolic mission of the whole people of God.

2. We acknowledge that in each of our Churches the Word of God is authentically preached and the sacraments of baptism and holy communion authentically administered according to the command of Christ.

3. We acknowledge that both our Churches share in a common faith set forth in the scriptures and summarised in the historic creeds.

4. We acknowledge our common inheritance in traditions of spirituality and liturgy .We rejoice in our diversity from which we may mutually benefit as we continue to develop varied forms of worship as appropriate to different situations.

5. We acknowledge each other's ordained ministries as given by God and as instruments of his grace by which our Churches are served and built up. As pilgrims together, we look forward to the time when our ministries can be fully interchangeable and our Churches visibly united.

6. We acknowledge that personal, collegial and comunnal oversight is embodied and practised in both

Churches, as each seeks to express continuity of apostolic life, mission and ministry.

Therefore :

We believe that God is calling our two Churches to a fuller relationship in which we commit ourselves:

- to share a common life and mission.
- to grow together so that unity may be visibly realized.

As the next steps towards that goal, we agree:

1. To pray for and with one another and to avail of every opportunity to worship together;

2. To welcome one another's members to receive Holy Communion and other ministries as appropriate;

3. To share resources in order to strengthen the mission of the Church;

4. To help our members to appreciate and draw out the gifts which each of our traditions has to offer the whole people of God;

5. To encourage the invitation of authorised persons of each Church to minister in the other Church, as far as the current disciplines of both Churches permit;

6. (a) To encourage united Methodist/Church of Ireland congregations:

   (i) where there are joint Church schemes,

(ii) where new churches are to be planted,

(iii) where local congregations wish to move in this direction;

(b) To encourage united Methodist / Church of Ireland chaplaincy work;

7. To enable a measure of joint training of candidates for ordained and lay ministries of our Churches where possible and appropriate and to encourage mutual understanding at all levels in our Churches;

8. To establish appropriate forms of consultation on matters of faith and order, mission and service;

9. To participate as observers by invitation in each other's forms of governance at every possible level;

10. To learn more about the practice of oversight in each other's Churches in order to achieve a fuller sharing of ministries at a later stage of our relationship.

APPENDIX

Celebrating the Covenant

The Chrome Hill Worship,
Lambeg, Lisburn, County Antrim,
26 September 2002

Welcome and Introduction

The grace of our Lord Jesus Christ, the love
of God, and the fellowship of the Holy Spirit
be with you all
And also with you.
God's love has been shed abroad in our
hearts
Through the Holy Spirit he has given us
Thanks be to God.

Reading: Ephesians 4:1–13

Hymn: Thou God of truth and love

Thou God of truth and love,
We seek thy perfect way,
Ready thy choice to approve,
Thy providence to obey;
Enter into thy wise design,
And sweetly lose our will in thine.

Why hast thou cast our lot
In the same age and place,
And why together brought
To see each other's face,
To join with loving sympathy
And mix our friendly souls in thee?

Didst thou not make us one
That we might one remain,
Together travel on,
And share our joy and pain,
Till all thy utmost goodness prove,
And rise renewed in perfect love ?

O may thy Spirit seal
Our souls unto that day,
With all thy fullness fill,
And then transport away :
Away to our eternal rest,
Away to our Redeemer's breast.

Charles Wesley (1707-88)

Prayers:
We confess that we have not loved each
other as you have loved us
Lord, have mercy

We have not made full use of those things
which have drawn us together and we have
cherished those things which have held us
apart
Christ, have mercy

We have been slow to respond to your call to
unity and mission together
Lord, have mercy

In your goodness you have offered us the forgiveness of our sins, and have held before us
the vision of new life
Blessed be God for ever

You have called us to a pilgrimage of reconciliation
Guide our feet in the ways of truth and love

You, O God, are the goal of our journey
Let your light shine upon our path

Let us pray together:

> Lord God our Father, you have called us into your family by the redeeming love of your Son and in the power of the Holy Spirit.
>
> Before you we recognize each other as brothers and sisters in Christ. Strengthen, we pray, the ties that bind us together in faith and love, and our commitment to travel together the pilgrim path of service and witness. Let our worship be in sincerity of word and action, and our end be the glory of the Lord.

> Our Father in heaven
> hallowed be your name,
> your kingdom come,
> your will be done,
> on earth as in heaven.
> Give us today our daily bread.
> Forgive our sins
> as we forgive those who sin against us.
> Save us from the time of trial
> and deliver us from evil.

For the kingdom, the power and the glory
are yours,
now and for ever.

AMEN

'The best of all is - God is with us'

Further details of the ongoing work of the Covenant
Council, and all relevant documents can be accessed
through the Council's website:
http://www.covenantcouncil.com/